RATTLESNAKES

BY S.L. HAMILTON

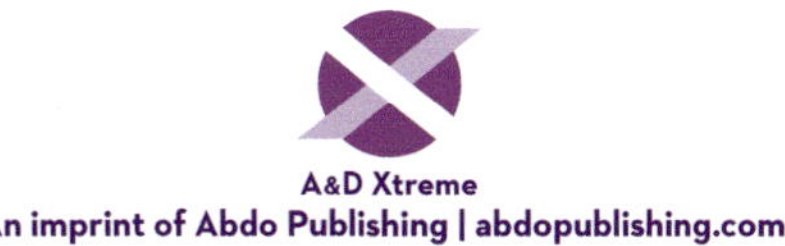

A&D Xtreme
An imprint of Abdo Publishing | abdopublishing.com

abdopublishing.com

Published by Abdo Publishing, a division of ABDO, PO Box 398166, Minneapolis, Minnesota 55439. Copyright ©2019 by Abdo Consulting Group, Inc. International copyrights reserved in all countries. No part of this book may be reproduced in any form without written permission from the publisher. A&D Xtreme™ is a trademark and logo of Abdo Publishing.

Printed in China.
022018
092018

Editor: John Hamilton
Copy Editor: Bridget O'Brien
Graphic Design: Sue Hamilton
Cover Design: Candice Keimig and Pakou Moua
Cover Photo: iStock
Interior Photos & Illustrations: Alamy-pgs 18, 20-21 & 29 (top); AP-pgs 24-25; Dreamstime-pg 28; Galileo Ramos-pgs 6-7; iStock-pgs 1 & 29 (bottom); Minden Pictures-pgs 4-5, 8-9, 14-15 & 16-17; National Geographic-pgs 7 (inset) & 27; Science Source-pgs 10-11, 12 & 26; Shutterstock-pgs 2-3, 6 (inset), 13, 19, 22-23 & 32; Wikimedia-pg 17 (inset).

Library of Congress Control Number: 2017963890
Publisher's Cataloging-in-Publication Data
Names: Hamilton, S.L., author.
Title: Rattlesnakes / by S.L. Hamilton.
Description: Minneapolis, Minnesota : Abdo Publishing, 2019. | Series: Xtreme snakes | Includes online resources and index.
Identifiers: ISBN 9781532116049 (lib.bdg.) | ISBN 9781532156977 (ebook)
Subjects: LCSH: Rattlesnakes--Juvenile literature. | Poisonous snakes--Juvenile literature. | Snakes--Juvenile literature. | Reptiles--Juvenile literature. | Herpetology--Juvenile literature.
Classification: DDC 597.964--dc23

CONTENTS

RATTLESNAKES

A rattlesnake's warning sound is so familiar that most people and animals know it means danger! However, a rattlesnake may not rattle until after it has struck. It may not even rattle at all. With or without a warning, its bite causes instant pain.

Rattlesnake venom can kill within seconds
or days, depending on the size of the victim.
But rattlesnakes are an important part of our
world. These shy but fearsome snakes are both
terrifying and amazing.

*Prairie
Rattlesnake*

BODY PARTS

Rattlesnakes have eyes with vertical pupils, like most venomous snakes. Non-venomous snakes usually have round pupils.

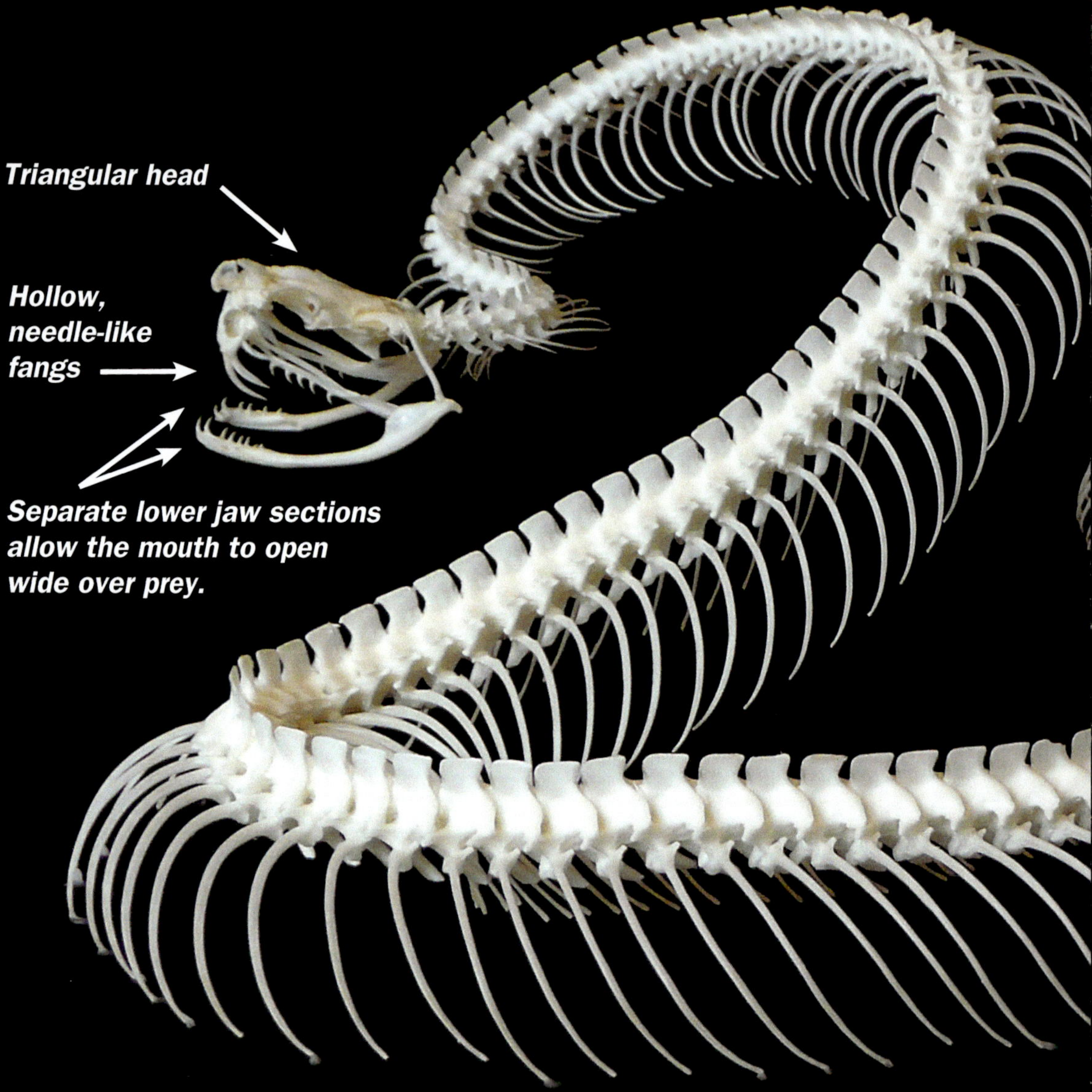

Triangular head

Hollow, needle-like fangs

Separate lower jaw sections allow the mouth to open wide over prey.

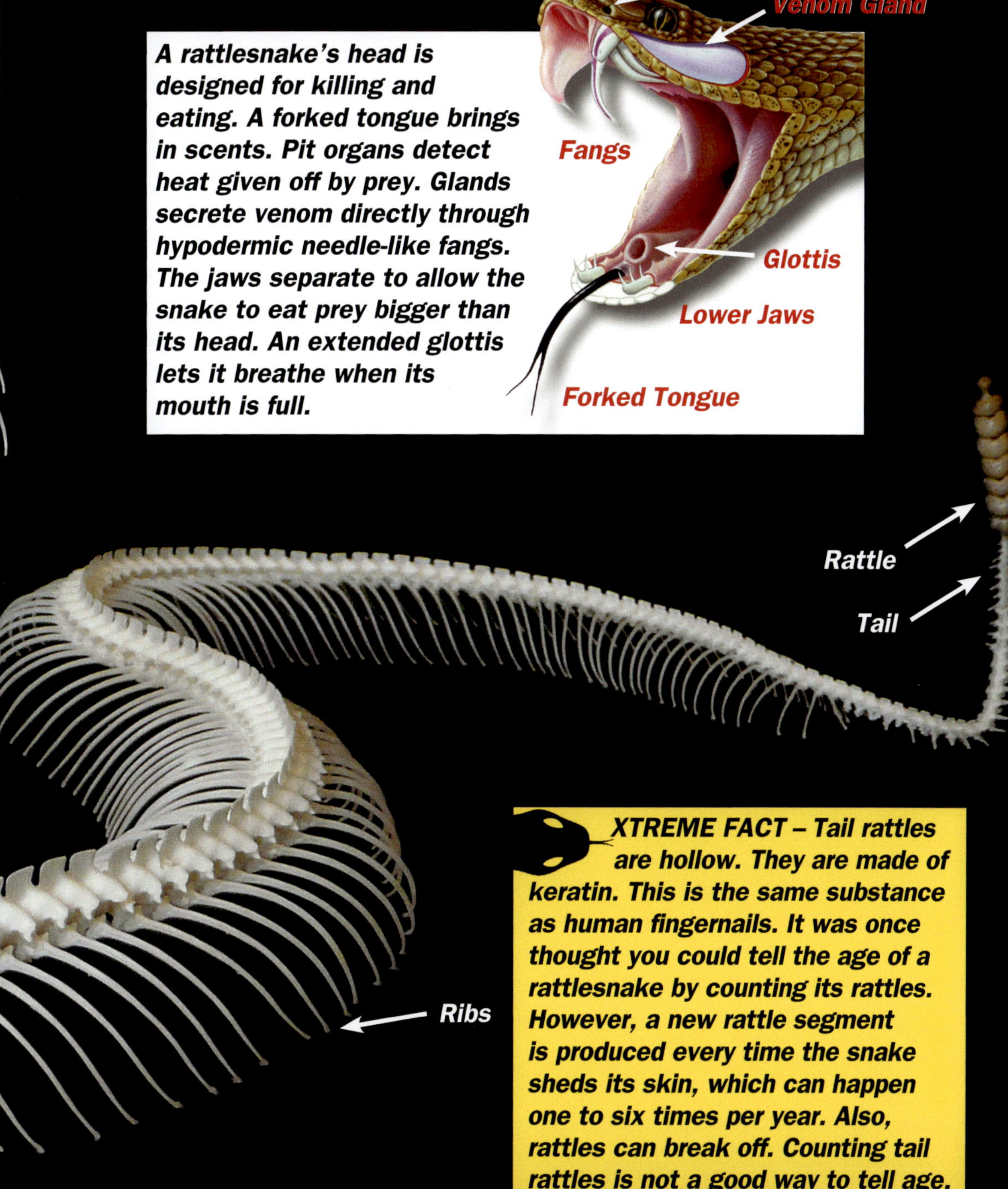
A rattlesnake's head is designed for killing and eating. A forked tongue brings in scents. Pit organs detect heat given off by prey. Glands secrete venom directly through hypodermic needle-like fangs. The jaws separate to allow the snake to eat prey bigger than its head. An extended glottis lets it breathe when its mouth is full.
Venom Gland
Fangs
Glottis
Lower Jaws
Forked Tongue
Rattle
Tail
Ribs
XTREME FACT – Tail rattles are hollow. They are made of keratin. This is the same substance as human fingernails. It was once thought you could tell the age of a rattlesnake by counting its rattles. However, a new rattle segment is produced every time the snake sheds its skin, which can happen one to six times per year. Also, rattles can break off. Counting tail rattles is not a good way to tell age.

Fangs and Venom

Rattlesnakes have an unlimited number of fangs and other teeth. When one falls out, another replaces it. Rattlesnakes lose their teeth frequently. A tooth may break off or stick in struggling prey. If this happens, there is another tooth behind it waiting to grow in.

Rattlesnake venom flows through hollow fangs and into the victim. The venom causes immediate pain at the bite site. Depending on the species of rattlesnake, the venom may destroy the target's blood, muscle, and tissue. Some rattlesnake venom attacks the prey's nervous system. This causes blindness and difficulty moving, swallowing, and breathing.

Eastern Diamondback Rattlesnake

PREY AND HUNTING

Depending on where they live, rattlesnakes eat mice, rats, gophers, squirrels, rabbits, birds, lizards, and sometimes large insects. Rattlesnakes are not scavengers. They hunt live creatures, but wait until their venom has killed the prey before swallowing it.

A rattlesnake uses heat-seeking sensors called pit organs to find prey. They "see" the victim's warmth. A rattler also uses its forked tongue to hunt. The tongue flicks out to pick up scent molecules on the ground and in the air. It then brings the "smells" back into the top of the mouth to the Jacobson's organ. This organ analyzes the odors and sends the information to the brain.

Prairie Rattlesnake

HABITAT

There are 36 species of rattlesnakes. They live in North, Central, and South America, but are mainly found in the southern United States. Depending on the species, rattlers may live in deserts, forests, cliffs, grasslands, swamps, and most places where their food can be found.

Sidewinder in a California desert.

In cold areas, rattlers hibernate during the winter. In places that get very hot, rattlesnakes go to shady dens, often in breaks between rocks.

A black-tailed rattlesnake stays cool under rocks.

Nesting

Like most reptiles, rattlesnakes begin life in an egg. However, a mother rattlesnake does not lay eggs. Instead, the eggs hatch inside the mother. She then gives birth to 5 to 10 live young. This is called being "ovoviviparous."

A timber rattlesnake mother with a nest of newborns.

Babies are born ready to hunt. They have fangs, venom, and all the senses needed to find prey. This is important since most rattlesnake mothers do not stay with their young. Some care for their newborns for a week. At this point, the young shed their first skin and start hunting.

Largest Rattlers

The eastern diamondback is the largest species of rattlesnake. It can grow to a length of 8 feet (2.4 m) and may weigh up to 10 pounds (4.5 kg). These huge snakes live in dry areas of the southeastern United States. Eastern diamondbacks are venomous. They are dangerous, but try to stay away from humans. If disturbed, their loud tail rattle is a clear warning.

Eastern Diamondback Rattlesnake

XTREME FACT –
American Revolutionary War General Christopher Gadsden designed one of the United States' first military flags. It featured an eastern diamondback rattlesnake ready to strike. He added a warning to England: Don't Tread On Me. (Don't step on the rights of Americans.)

DONT TREAD ON ME

SMALLEST RATTLERS

The pygmy rattlesnake is one of the smallest rattlesnakes. Adults grow to a length of 14 to 22 inches (36 to 56 cm). They are found in the southeastern United States. They live in burrows made by gopher tortoises or rodents. They eat small mammals, birds, lizards, insects, and frogs. Because these rattlers are small, they produce and inject less venom. It is unlikely that their bite could kill a human.

The desert massasauga grows to a length of 21 inches (53 cm). These small rattlers make their homes in desert areas of the southern United States and northern Mexico. Although they live in hot areas, they do not like the heat. They are most active at night when they hunt for mice, lizards, and frogs.

Desert Massasauga

19

Fastest Striker

A rattlesnake will strike to hunt or to protect itself. It does so with unbelievable speed. A western diamondback rattlesnake was clocked striking at a target at 915 feet per second (279 meters per second).

Western Diamondback Rattlesnake

XTREME FACT – Rattlesnakes strike their targets in 50 to 90 milliseconds. Humans blink their eyes in 300 to 400 milliseconds, or about 1/3 to 1/2 second. So it's possible for a human to blink and not see a rattlesnake strike.

Rattlesnakes are very accurate from a coiled or semi-coiled position. The coiled position keeps more of its body protected. A rattler can strike a target one-third to one-half the length of the snake itself. So a 3-foot (1 m) snake can reach a victim up to 1.5 feet (.5 m) away.

Deadliest Rattlesnakes

The Mojave rattlesnake has the most toxic venom of any rattlesnake. The venom is both a hemotoxin and a neurotoxin. A hemotoxin causes blood and body parts to die and decay, like most rattlesnake venom. But Mojave venom is also a neurotoxin. It interferes with the information sent from a creature's brain to its muscles and body parts. The venom quickly stops a victim from being able to move or even breathe.

Mojave Rattlesnake

SNAKE HANDLERS

Most humans try to stay far away from rattlesnakes. But some people handle rattlesnakes in their work. Technicians "milk" venom from rattlesnakes. The venom is used to make antivenin to treat people who have been bitten by a rattlesnake. Wildlife removal experts are trained to capture and take away dangerous pests, such as snakes. Herpetologists go to college to learn about reptiles and amphibians. They work for zoos and museums, as well as companies that do research and environmental studies. Some entertainers use rattlesnakes in their shows. This is dangerous and often an unfit life for a rattlesnake.

An eastern diamondback
rattlesnake is milked for
its venom.

If You Are Bitten

If you are bitten by a rattlesnake, it is important to follow these steps:

1) Get medical help IMMEDIATELY. Go right away, but walk. Get to a hospital as quickly as you can.

2) Stay calm. This keeps the heart from beating fast and spreading the venom quickly throughout the body. Remember: The bite may have been a dry bite with no venom.

3) Look closely at the snake's markings or get a picture of it. If you can identify what type of snake it is, doctors will know what antivenin to use.

The best defense against a rattlesnake bite is to *not* get bitten. If you are in places where there are rattlesnakes, be very aware of your surroundings. Watch where you are stepping or sitting. Wear hiking boots and loose pants to keep a snake's fangs from reaching you. Hike with a buddy so he or she can get help if you can't hike out.

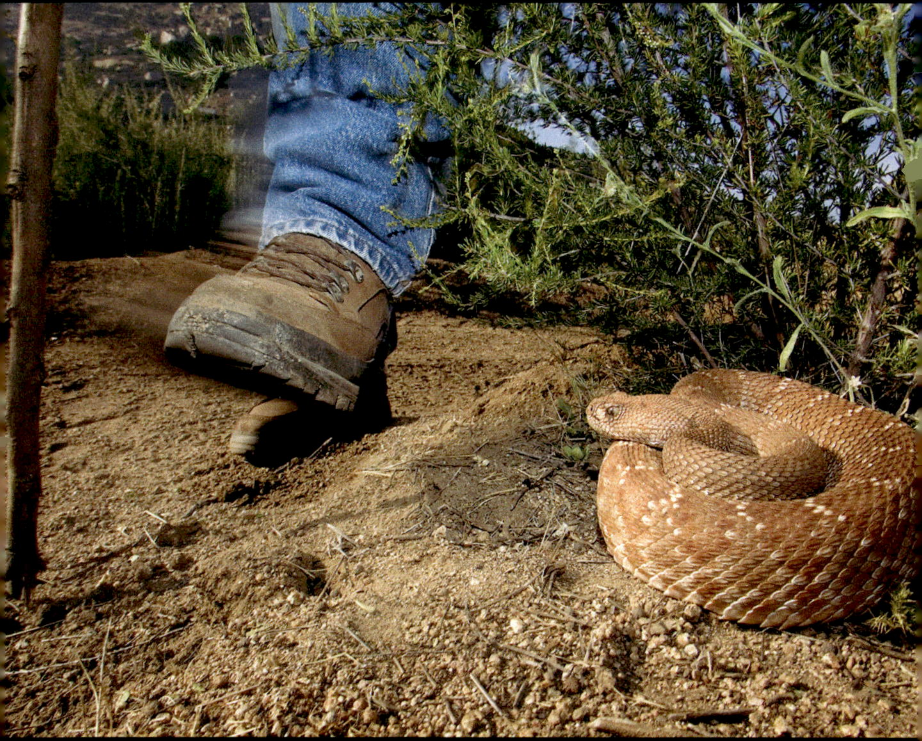

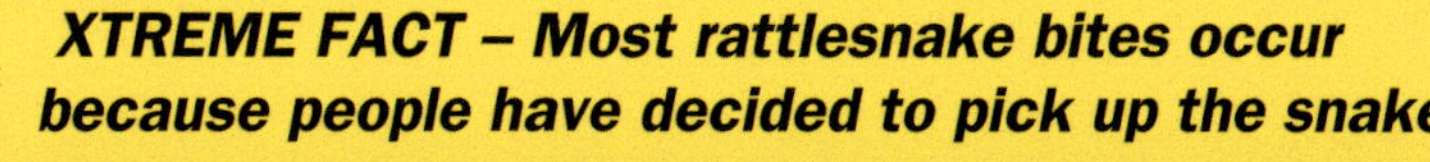

Are They Endangered?

Three rattlesnake species are listed as threatened by the U.S. Fish and Wildlife Service. They are the Aruba Island rattlesnake, the eastern massasauga rattlesnake, and the New Mexican ridge-nosed rattlesnake. The eastern diamondback may be added to this list.

Loss of habitat is causing many rattlesnake deaths. Rattlesnakes do not want to be near humans. Humans do not want rattlesnakes near them. But rattlesnakes are important to keep a balance in nature. Without them, rodents and other pests would grow in numbers. Maintaining a good rattlesnake population, while keeping people safe, is important to our world.

GLOSSARY

ANTIVENIN
Also called antivenom. A liquid used to treat and stop the effects of a bite from venomous creatures, such as snakes. Antivenin is created by injecting an animal or eggs with a small amount of a specific snake's venom. The host animal produces antibodies against the venom, which can then be taken from its blood and used to treat humans.

GLOTTIS
A tube-like opening that brings air to a rattlesnake's lungs. The glottis can move to one side or another, allowing the rattlesnake to breathe when its mouth is full.

HEMOTOXIN
A substance, such as rattlesnake venom, that attacks a victim's blood and organs. Once injected into the body, a hemotoxin destroys red blood cells and the body's tissues and organs. It is painful and can kill in a short time.

HYPODERMIC NEEDLE
A hollow needle used to inject fluid under the skin.

JACOBSON'S ORGAN
A sensory organ that snakes use to smell their prey.

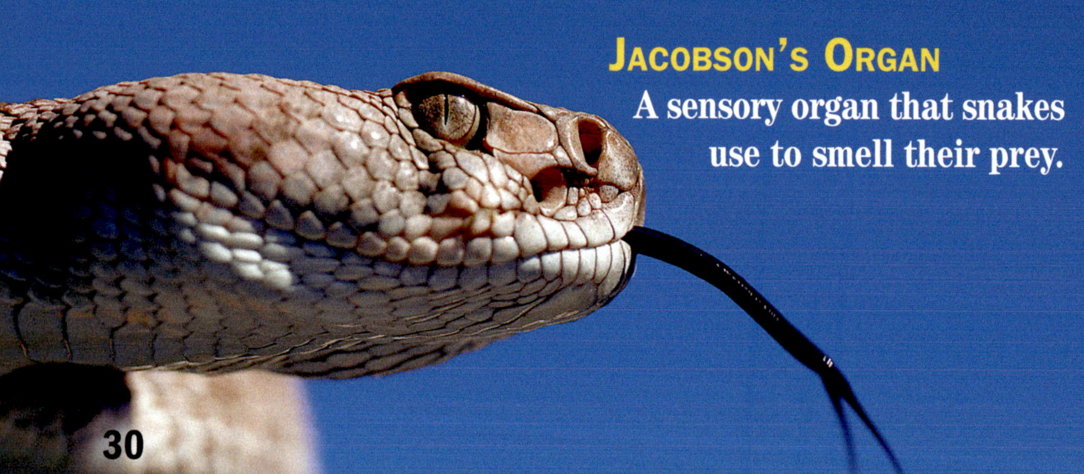

NEUROTOXIN

A substance, such as some snake venom, that attacks the victim's nervous system. Once injected into the body, a neurotoxin prevents the brain from sending messages to the rest of the body. A neurotoxin stops brain signals to the muscles. The body cannot move and the lungs cannot breathe. Death can come quickly.

PUPIL

The black part in the middle of the eye that opens and closes to let in more or less light. In rattlesnakes, the pupils are shaped like vertical slits. In humans, pupils are round.

SCAVENGER

Creatures that eat what they find, including dead and dying prey.

TOXIC

Poisonous and sometimes deadly. Snake venom is toxic.

VENOM

A toxic liquid that some animals such as rattlesnakes, Gila monsters, and scorpions use for killing prey and for defense.

ONLINE RESOURCES

To learn more about rattlesnakes, visit abdobooklinks.com. These links are routinely monitored and updated to provide the most current information available.